Rainbow Love

Written By: Melissa Edmunds

Copyright 2012

ISBN 978-1-300-22457-0

Contents

Locked Heart
Love Her
Love 2
Love Is...
Love Is
Love
Me Without
Mine Babe
My Wish
Need You
No I Without You
One Mother
One Who Always Loves You
Only Love You
Perfect
Poets Love
Racism
Rednecks
Rolling Stone
Saving Angel
Sex
She Is
Special Delivery
Staring At You
Teardrops
Tears
The Night Before
The Teapot
True Love
Uncharted Ground
Valentine
Wet
What I Love
Whenever
Whole
Wish You Were Here
Without You
Womens Moods
You Kissed Me
You Showed Me Love
You
Your Life

A KISS FROM A GIRAFFE

I got a kiss
from a giraffe.
He tickled my ear
it made me laugh.
It made me so happy
that I could cry.
My greatest experience
I cannot lie.
I gave him some water
he licked from my cap.
My life was perfect
but then I woke up.

A TASTE OF YOU

I need to take you in my strong arms
let me hold you oh so close and tight
our sighs rising high into the heavens
rocking wrapped up in sweet delight.

You know I'll never ever let you go
I yearn to kiss your lush warm lips
till we melt blissful in love's wild fire
in a dance eternal, joined at the hip.

I want you to know my heart's pure voice
hear me pour out my feelings for you
to shout them at the boundless sky
so strong, so deep, so clear, so true.

Love's feast calls us to this moment
no reason needed, for what we do
I have a gnawing hunger in my soul
always aching for just a taste of you.

AFTERLIFE

You are so beautiful,
and way to nice.

I love you once, I love you twice.

I'll scream I love you
with my last breath.

Even in the afterlife, I'll love you to death.

ANGEL IN ME

Some people believe, there is a one
the one who points, your way to the sun.
A person they believe, makes them complete
the one who will support, when facing defeat.

'You are my Angel', my one and only
my forever love, so we'll never be lonely.
You've brought to my life, all your love and care
it made me see, when I realized how rare..
It is to meet your Angel, or their lifetime one
through you and my children, whose life has begun.

What you've done, you've illuminated my soul
it's you and your love, that has made me whole.
The feel of your love, that has made me whole.
The feel of your love, your soft touch and caress
we're tight so close, your heart beats in my chest.

All that we have, always felt missing before
though I love you today, tomorrow it will be more.
Our love is life, we are the strongest tree
which will always grow forever, like you and me.

You have opened my heart and held it so dear
you are my Angel and will always keep it near.
You have seen my ups and cared when I was low.
'You are my Angel', I just need you to know.

You entered my life, through a ray of sun above
and when we leave, we will leave together in love.
My love for you, has become my reason to be
I hope one day you'll find, your Angel in me.

AS IF....

Touch yourself...
touch it as if...
as if the moon and stars collided in a
fantastic fireworks display for your insides only.

as if...
the most exhilerating part of your self...
expression is between your thighs
as if your fingers where my eyes...

touch it as if...
it were my warm hands gliding down
your cool flesh removing your inhibitions
one stitch at a time and dropping it delicately to the floor...
imagine my caring caress
on your cheek,
my breath on your neck,
my kiss on that secret place that...
shhh! only I know.

as if...
I was kissing your soul
and the explosion flooded the nile.

as if...
I were licking your wounds,
weary from battle dreched in perspiration
and drowned in forgiveness and tears.

as if...
your dreams included mystical figures
that assumed postitions reminiscent of tribal war rituals
and danced around our room for your pleasure alone.

as if...
our brothers and sisters
that hung from southern trees
could feel the love from your blood drenched tears
and it would take away thier pain.

as if...
this planet were our private playground

and making love on Venus was as common as our bedroom.

as if...
the places you call home
only existed in my heart
and your only safe,
quiet place was in my arms.

as if...
"erotic" weren't nearly as intense a word
to describe these acts but,
merely as common a descriptive as "kiss" or "touch".

as if...
the moans would alert the universe
of our existence and the eruption of your passion
would render Mt. St. Helen powerless.

as if...
we were one day short
of our forever
and tomorrow did not exist for us
and yesterday faded with our last nights moon.

as if...
we were destined to never meet but,
live with the feeling of slipping time
and memories of what never existed
except here in our minds.

touch it...
as if...
those fantasies collided
and our dreams floated to the ceiling
and danced to the sound of the rhythm
that we alone have created.

as if...
I were laying near
and my touch melted your heart
and my kiss warmed your soul.

as if...
time were a mere technicality
that existed only for our amusement.

touch it...
as if...
I loved you forever
and infinity was too short a descriptive
for what we would face together.

as if...
your forever begins with the first touch.

touch yourself...
as if...
you could see the love I feel for you,
as clear as the stars in the sky
and never had to question my commitment to us.

touch yourself as if...
you were touching me...............

BEARS

I look out my window and what do I see?
A large grizzly bear coming to visit me.
Oh Lord, please change that bear's direction,
he's not invited and I don't want his affections.

I look again out my window and what do I see?
A large black bear standing next to an oak tree.
I was taught to be polite when company arrives,
but this uninvited guest has taken me by surprise.

I look again out my window and what do I see?
A large black bear preparing to take his leave.
There are many grizzly bears in these here hills,
but I ain't Goldie Locks and I don't want any porridge!

BELIEVE

Believe in love
Believe in faith
Believe in truth
Believe that no matter what happens, you have the power to prevail

Believe in strenght
Believe in courage
Believe in honor
Believe that everyone has the power to be good at heart

Believe in song
Believe in dance
Believe in culture
Believe that no matter who you are or where you're from - everyone is unique

Believe in things you never would
Believe in doing things you never could
Believe in achievement
Believe that if you think you can, you can - but if you think you can't, you won't

Believe in the damned
Believe in the degenerate
Believe in the corrupted
Believe that evil does exist in many forms, but all can be overcome

Believe in spiritual
Believe in holy
Believe in scared
Believe that your personal values can never be taken from you

Believe in mad
Believe in depressed
Believe in suicidal
Believe that one smile can save a life

Believe in magic
Believe in hope
Believe in dreams
Believe that the unbelievable happens everyday

Believe in time
Believe in forever

Believe in YOU
Believe that as long as you believe in yourself - anything is possible

BODY TO BODY

Roses are red, nuts are brown,
skirts go up, pants go down.
Body to body, skin to skin
when it's stiff stick it in.
It goes in dry and comes out wet.
the longer it's in, the stronger it gets.
It comes out dripping and starts to sag
but it's not what you think, it's a used tea bag!

BUTTERFLY FLICKS

Soft butterfly flicks almost silent
asking your lips if their wanting me more.
Soft and surreal, the moment of happening
in sensual kiss shared truths revealed to the core.

Soft butterfly flicks now faster,
your hand in my hair the most loving sensation.
Soft lips form an O and encircle and suck your nipples,
one tongue and now sotly two fingers.....elation.

Soft butterly flicks begging quivering eruption,
your hips push your mound into passion sustaining.
Soft permission to die for a moment,
your soul into mine as your tender warmths raining.

Soft butterfly flicks to your neck in consoling,
our hearts reassured, sincere cherished embrace.
Soft throbbing abating, still yearning,
complete adoration, spent bodies in grace.

CAPTURE

Listen to my heartbeat
let me breathe you in
absorbing your warmth.
My eyes burn desire
wanting to taste your kiss
your voice, honey to my ears.
My heart shudders,
my body trembles.
I could hold you forever
never wanting to let go.
Constantly caressing you,
fingers through your hair
brushing against your cheek.
My hands learning every curve
no need for sleep
just hold me tightly
and capture my heart,
as you have captivated me.

CATCH MY BREATH

It's late at night,
but the weather couldn't be more perfect.
I'm half naked,
but you mirror me.

We begin slowly,
but soon enough we pick up the pace.
Adrenaline shoots through my veins
like a drug...
I think I'm addicted.

My chest begins to hurt
from the up and down motion
and I'm starting to gasp for air.

We slow it down a little bit.
You're breathing heavily,
and sweat covers your chest.

"Don't stop" you say with broken breaths....

My entire body is numb at this point,
but I don't want to stop...
Not yet at least.

The only thing keeping me going
is knowing we only have a half a mile left...
That's only two more laps.
Then I can catch my breath.

COMPLETE

Passion in your kisses,
when you come to visit.
My day always gets better and
no one matters but you.

Every moment filled with the
most romance anyone can dream about.
When we first met I tried to close my heart
and you got me to open up again.

There is nowhere in this would
I want to be, only waking up to
your beautiful face and to the person
that makes me feel loved and complete.

CRAYOLAS

My mom bought me crayons
to learn how to draw,
it's not really my thing
but she laid down the law.

She said to go get them
from off of the shelf,
they'll help me improve
expressing myself.

She bought me the biggest
box that they had.
It has every color
I think even plaid.

There's salmon and orchid
and all sorts of yellow,
eggplant, sherbert,
and mountain mellow.

Asparagus, mint,
maroon and mulberry,
tickle me pick,
and even strawberry.

Almond and lime,
green apple and plum,
there might even be one
the shade of my bum.

Sunset, moon glow,
and radical red,
magenta, blue wonder,
and also rye bread.

Turquoise, and rose,
and purple pizzazz,
but that's still not all
the colors it has.

Tumbleweed, carrot,
and tangerine,

jazzberry jam
and a new olive green.

Now I could keep going
for a day and a year,
but I think that is all
that I'll make you hear.

I've still got the rest
of the story to tell
and I can't say lately
I'm feeling that well.

When my mom came back
to see what I'd done,
I could tell right away
she was proud of me.

Tears of joy filled her eyes
like I knew they would,
as I showed her my list
of the ones that taste good!

DEATH DO US PART

My heart is yours, to have and to hold.
'Til death do us part, is how its been told.
My love is grand, so tender, so sweet.
You were in my dreams, that's where we first met.
Please promise forever you will always hold.
My arms are strong, so truthful, so bold.
'Til death do us part, will always be told.

DEFINE LOVE

so how do you define love?
is it the subtle way you look at each other?
or just the way you smile?
is it the way your bodies move together?
or just being able to hold hands?

how do you define real love?
being able to finish each others sentences?
or just knowing what you're both thinking?
is it all the fancy dates you've had?
or just being able to stay home together?

how do you define endless love?
is it all the days lived together?
or the minutes you've missed each other?
is it the health you've shared?
or all the pain and sorrow you've been through?
so how do you define love?

DESIRE

In the still of the evening
without sunlight to intrude.
I see the twilight in your eyes
as the moon sets up the mood.

Playing music soft and low
while romance fills the air.
I can't help but feel aroused
the very moment you come near.

You submit to my embrace
while candles flick their flame.
The smell of sweet perfume
seems to drive my lust insane.

As I look into your eyes
and run my fingers through your hair.
I taste the sweetness of your neck
as I nibble at your ear.

I then whisper words of love
as you answer with a sigh.
In a very sexy way
your sweet body comes alive.

Your the heat of my desire
as we slowly come undressed.
I then start to lay you down
while you welcome my caress.

With your luscious sexy curves
you have a taste I can't resist.
Your breasts show some response
when I touch them with a kiss.

As I soak inside your love
to a sexy love condition.
Feeling passions start to rise
while making love in all positions.

You give me so much pleasure
for ecstasy is here.

With you wrapped inside my arms
to this heated love we share.

Now no one can come close
to this love that we inspire.
For only you can fill this joy
and the heat of my desire.

DOWN UNDER

Down under was a quiet girl named Paula
who couldn't find a man to make her holla,
then she tumbled for a Sheila
and became a sudden squeala.
Now she tells the fellas not to even call her!

EVERY BREATH

With every breath you take, my lungs fill with air,
I crave your solidarity this silence I can't bare,
every time your heart beats blood rushes through my veins,
without you everything even my happiness wanes,
as you fall asleep I find it hard to open my eyes,
every other feminine smile my heart denies,
the water you drink soothes my throat,
all the letters at your door I wrote,
my life will continue this way,
one last thing I wish to say,
a thought I've thought everyday,
when you pass away,
will I be okay?

EVERYTHING BUT YOU

I want to be invaded
where resistance is futile,
against her on rushing passion.
I want to be devoured by her lust,
        and my own.
I want to be striped of civility
and social contrivance.
I want the sight of me to fill her eyes with hunger.
I want to smell the wanting,
taste it, as I lick the sweat from her body,
bared fangs seeking flesh.
My whole world destroyed and created by the tip of her tongue
moving inside me.
My body hers,
realeasing the torrent that's been held for a lifetime.
        Take me,
        enter me,
        feel me from the inside,
        move with me,
        against me,
        faster and harder,
        longer and longer,
until I forget everything but you.

FIRST TIME

I want to know you
I want to touch you
I want to love you.

A silent room bathed in moonlight,
barefoot move toward the bed,
lips touching,
tongues tasting on soft, anxious breath.

Soft skin meeting softness,
the Goddess smiles.

FISH

I knew a lady trapper
who would trap out in the sticks.
She used to be a flapper
back in nineteen twenty-six.

I met her in a diner
well not really just a bar,
and I told her I'm a miner
as she puffed on her cigar.

She said your kinda ugly
and your breath stinks awlful bad,
but I been fussin with my fugly
so, I'll tell you why I'm sad.

See I love to hunt for beaver,
it's my passion I can't lie,
but I left my love's receiver
cuz she wouldn't eat beaver pie.

Now I could have dried some jerky,
guess I sould have fried some pork,
but my beaver tastes so perky
fugly wouldn't touch her fork.

Well, I miss her, I'm lonely
she's my only, what a dish.
I can't leave her over beaver,
so from now on its tuna fish!

FLOWERS

It's sunny outside and the air is clean.
It's a good day to go.
We can run in the fields,
and pick the flowers.
It's a good day to go.
The sky is blue and I grab your hand,
I won't leave 'til I taste your lips again.
I can tell by your eyes,
a pure surprise,
something waiting for me.

The smell is sweet,
quite unique.
My obsession with you
is what dreamers dream.
Beyong all reason,
no way to awake,
I lie under you.

One heart and one mind,
we are tied to this,
never to be alone.
I love what you show me,
every night we love.
I kiss your lips once more
in these fields of flowers.

FRECKLES

I want to be your freckles,
so, then I'm always near.
I want to be your feckles,
oh yes, please my dear.

To be the freckles on your arms,
feel you wrapped in me all night long.

To be the freckle on your nose,
all day look into your eyes.

To be the set on your back,
that makes the perfect set.

To be that special freckle,
all the way there.

To be that freckle of all the rest,
to be that freckle would be the best!

FRIEND

When life gets you down,
and there's nowhere to turn,
I'll help you through and
I'll share your concern.

I'll try my best to return every favor,
when you're sure that you'll drown,
the I'll be your lifesaver,
even if we both go down.

Whether we sink or swim
doesn't matter at all,
just know that I'll be there
whenever you call.

I'll pull you out
when life pulls you under.
I'll be the sun
when there's lightning and thunder.

And when it's all over
and we've fought every war,
there's one thing I promise,
of this I am sure,
when the time comes
that we're put to our rest,
be sure that you know that
my friend, you're the best.

And if there is Heaven,
then I know you'll be there,
that if you die first
then you'll hear every prayer.
And soon I'll join you,
but just know until then,
that I'll miss you each day
'til I see you again.

At the end of the tunnel,
you'll be my guiding light,
you'll lead me to Heaven
away from the night.

We'll be there together,
and we'll never grow old.
And we'll walk hand in hand
on the streets paved of gold.

FUNNY...NOT...

it's funny how hello is always accompanied with goodbye
it's funny how good memories can start to make you cry
it's funny how forever never seems to last
it's funny how much you'd lose if you forgot about your past
it's funny how "friends" can just leave when you are down
it's funny how when you need someone they are never around
it's funny how people change and think they're so much better
it's funny how many lies are packed into one "love letter"
it's funny how one night can contain so much regret
it's funny how you can forgive but not forget
it's funny how ironic life turns out to be
but the funniest part of all, is none of that's funny to me.

GONE AWAY

An Angel whispered
take my hand and
come with me
you're work here is done.

I went away to a place
where there's no tears, nor sorrow
only laughter and smiles,
there will always be a tomorrow.

As I move amongst the clouds.
I'll look down and smile upon you,
while the Angels
sing a heavenly song.

I am not alone
all who went before
are here
they awaited my return.

I know you'll grieve
and wish I was still here
I am here in the memories
you hold dear.

Remember how much I
love you
and know I took your
love with me.

I did not wish for
you to cry, nor feel sad.
My pain is gone and
I am free!

Soon you'll come to me
until then
God will be with you
just as He's with me.

HEART

Do you like heart shapes,
as I do,
that come in every size and
rainbow hue?

Do you like pink ones,
green, or blue?
A bunch of hearts
or just a few?

A heart is such
a pretty shape.
Reminding us to love,
and not hate.

I think that hearts
are nice to see.
If I had four
I'd give you three.

HER TRUST

As you slept I could not
I stood trembling, lost in thought

You on one side, me on the other
yet I blushed when I pulled back the covers

I slid in carefully under the sheets
praying our skin would not touch or meet

My heart racing out of control
wanting to have you, wanting to hold

Feeling every vein in my body pulse with that relentless beat
like a volcano wanting to erupt, surging with heat

Pulling the pillows and the sheets up tight
feeling the urge to flee or fight

No where to run, no where to hide
trying to fight this need inside

I've overcome this battle of pain and lust
and won something more important, her trust

HER

Her eyes so beautiful,
I love her so much,
she gives me faith
in life again.

One kiss from her
and I melt, as I know
the passion between
us will never go.

HOOKED

You hold the key
to my heart.
You held it
from the very start.

All it took
was just one look,
and I was hooked
on you.

HOW I HUNGER

Warm breeze blows into the bedroom window,
the moon is pouring over us in a silver wave.
Aching I watch it's flowing gentle movement,
rippling slowly over your pale smooth skin.

The beauty of your glowing body beckons me
to touch, to taste, to love its graceful expanse,
from your forehead to toes, fingers to nose,
how I hunger to know you so completely.

To gladly find all the wondrous places
that bring you such sweet pleasure.
Forging bonds that tie your heart to mine,
two hearts beating wildly together as one.

HUG

Your arms around me
just holding on so lovingly
neither one of us saying anything
and neither one of us needing to
I could stay like this forever
nothing else could begin to feel this good.

Your hair tickles my nose and I don't care
it's just another chance to breathe you in
to feel your warmth and perfect softness
and I really do love it when you sigh to me
I understand exactly what you are saying
and if there is a chance I forgot today
to tell you that I love you
and I need you so
I truly do,
love to hug you.

I CHOOSE

Honey,
if love comes in colors,
I choose blue.

If love comes in flowers,
I'll choose a rose.

If love comes in songs,
I'll think of choosing blues.

But if love should come in human beings,
I'll definitely not think twice before
I'll choose you!

I WANT YOU.......

I want you in my arms,
against my body,
all alone,
just you and I wrapped in each others souls.

I want to kiss you,
all over,
all night,
until morning comes.

I want to make love with you,
for ever and ever,
over and over,
until the world is no more.

I want to love you,
with all my heart,
with all my soul,
'til we are no more.

I want you....
        ...I just hope you want me also!

I WISH

I lie on the ground
and stare into space.
The stars start to move
into the shape of your face.

I see you there now
looking down at me,
with that cute little smirk
that I like to see.

You say, "close your eyes",
"tell me what you see."
I see only two people
just you and me.

We're walking the shoreline
with our feet getting wet.
The horizon turns pink
as the sun starts to set.

Oh, I wish I could be
in that one special place,
as I lie on the ground
and stare into space.

IF WORDS COULD EXPLAIN

If words could explain
how much you mean to me.
If words could explain
how your love has set me free.

If words could explain
all the feeling that I've felt.
If words could explain
I know your heart would melt.

If words could explain
how I'll never let you go.
If words could explain
then everyone would know.

If words could explain
how you're my Angel from up above.
If words could explain,
then they wouldn't doubt our love.

If words could explain
these feelings within my soul.
If words could explain
how you've somehow made me whole.

If words could explain
every dream I've dreamed of you.
If words could explain
how I know our love is true.

If words could explain
then you would know how much I care.
If words could explain
you would know I'll always be there.

If words could explain
that I've promised you my life.
If words could explain
how it feels to be you wife.

IF YOU ONLY KNEW

If you only knew
how much I really cared.
If you only knew
that deep inside I'm scared.

If you only knew
how much love I want to show.
If you only knew
I'll never let you go.

If you only knew
how you're always on my mind.
If you only knew
then the key to my heart you would find.

If you only knew
I think of you each day.
If you only knew
just how much I wanted to say.

If you only knew
that you were made just for me.
If you only knew
a brighter tomorrow we could see.

If you only knew
that we were made to be together.
If you only knew
that I want to be with you forever.

IN MY DREAMS

In my dreams,
I shed no tears.
In my dreams,
I have no fears.

In my dreams,
I find that place.
In my dreams,
I see your face.

In my dreams,
I found your heart.
In my dreams,
we're never apart.

In my dreams,
I wish I could stay.
In my dreams,
with you I lay.

In my dreams,
I hold you tight.
In my dreams,
each and every night.

In my dreams,
these feelings so deep.
In my dreams,
you'll always keep.

In my dreams,
we'll forever be free.
In my dreams,
you and me forever.

JUST A TOUCH

It starts with a touch,
  your nipples get hard.
It turns to a kiss,
  you start to get wet.
Clothes start to fall to the floor,
  you start to moan.
You barely make it to the bed,
  you beg for more.
We make love,
  the whole night through.
To think it all starts,
  with just a touch.

JUST THE BEGINING

I don't have much to give you
in the way of material things.
But then, I have never been a material person.....
So it wouldn't matter much anyway.
I do have something to give you, though...
and I hope you accept this git with joy.
I have chosen not to wrap it...
I want it to be presented to you
as prestine as can be.
And anyway, decorations or wrappings would
certainly ruin the effect.
And so it is...That I stand before you...
Unclothed, but surprisingly, unashamed
of my nakedness.
You have already captured a piece of my heart,
and you have captivated my soul.
The only thing left for me to present to you
is my very being...and I do that willingly,
happily, and most of all...lovingly.
Standing before you...watching your every movement...
Seeing the desire in your eyes
for the very first time.
I don't believe in all of my life,
I have never witnessed a moment
as beautiful as this.
Neither one of us can speak...
And we are finding, even breathing, is difficult.
Your heartbeat is pounding out a rhythm
that almost assaults my ears.
I can hear it from where I stand across from you...
And every beat speaks of your love for me.
I am giving you this gift tonight,
because I desperately want you to look inside.
I want you to open this package that I offer you,
slowly...lovingly...sensuously...
And search for what lies within.
You don't have to look far, you know...
Everything I feel for you is just below the surface.
So it shouldn't take long for you
to discover that beauty awaiting you there.
Go ahead...open this gift as a child would
on a snowy Christmas morning...

in a hurried fashion...rather like a frenzy, if you will.
But once that initial gift is opened...
And the passion subsides...
Please promise me
that gift of myself...
is only just the begining.

KEEP COOL

Brown grass cruches beneath my feet,
and pavement burns to the touch,
the sun is especially hot today,
take care not to get too much.
The river is so far from here,
and there is no good path.
So, I guess I'll go and get cool
in a refreshing bath.

LANGUAGE

Yvette, a friend,
likes to attend
a class (it keeps her young).
so last July
she thought she'd try
to learn another tongue.

They offered such
as french and dutch
but, on the page above
her eyes soon scanned
a course they planned,
entitled "Women's Love".

When we next met
I asked Yvette
to tell me how she found it.
Though not the worst,
she failed at first
to get her tongue around it.

But as the weeks
have passed, she seeks
the students who are single.
It clearly pays
for now she says
she's multi-(cunni)lingual.

LIFE & LIVING

Prison is for people
          who give up living
          and on reality.

The nuthouse is for people
          who can't handle life
          and living.

Marriage is for those of us
          who are somewhere inbetween.

LOCKED HEART

My heart has a door
that always stayed locked.
Its guarded by walls
of solid stone block.
My minds like a safe
with treasures inside.
It can not be cracked
no matter how hard you try.
You knocked down the stone,
and walked through the door,
taking over my heart
and making it yours.
You opened it up
and filled it with light.
From that second on
it was yours without fight.
So from this day forward
I will always be here,
to pick you up when you are down
and fill you with cheer.
As long as you know
no matter what gives,
that you are my heart
and I need you to live.

LOVE HER

How do you know you love her?

Well you,
       wine her,
       dine her,
       call her,
       support her,
       hold her,
       surprise her,
       compliment her,
       smile at her,
       listen to her,
       laugh with her,
       cry with her,
       romance her,
       encourage her,
       believe in her,
       pray with her,
       pray for her,
       cuddle with her,
       shop with her,
       give her jewelry,
       buy her flowers,
       hold her hand,
       write love letters to her,
       go to the end of the world and back again for her.

When you don't question it, you just do it that's when you know
       you love her!

LOVE IS.....

Love is gentle,
love is kind,
love is what I see
when I look in your eyes.

Love is calming,
love is soothing,
love is radiating
from all your beauty.

Love is caring,
love is sharing,
love is all consuming
in your presence.

Love is so many things,
to many to list.
Love is simply,
being with you.

LOVE IS.....

Love is a burning desire,
that makes your heart light on fire.
Love is being with you,
someone saying I love you too.

Love is your tender kiss,
something I don't want to miss.
Love is you and me,
and that is all I can see.

LOVE

Love is a cup of coffee, in the brisk morning glow.

Love is the hand of a child, warm and soft, filled with innocent affection.

Love is the broken, dripping sink, in a house built for two.

Love is a friday at 5 o'clock.

Love is a warm shoulder, protecting a tired head.

Love is 70's rock and skate shoes.

Love is the lonely, aching heart, rejected by the one it was gifted to.

Love is an entire day spent in bed, doing everything but sleeping.

Love is a song, felt deep within the soul.

Love is a pain, is many pains, in places you didn't even know you had.

Love is a knowing look, shared between lovers.

Love is a cup of tea, brewed by a friend.

Love is an evening at the beach, watching the sun dip out of sight.

Love is a quirky grin, meant only for one.

Love is anything but a four-letter word.

LOVE

Love...
        With all your heart and soul,
        as if there will be no tomorrow.

Love...
        With gentleness and kindness,
        as if you are mending a butterfly's broken wing.

Love...
        With honesty and trust,
        as if nothing could break your bond.

Love...
        With passion and fierceness,
        as if you were licking the wounds, weary from battle,
        drenched in perspiration and drowned in forgiveness and tears.

Love...
        No matter how you describe it, it is a precious thing,
        as if life depends upon it.

Love...
        Love...
            Love....

ME WITHOUT

Love me without fear,
trust me without questioning,
need me without demanding,
want me without restrictions,
accept me without change,
desire me without inhibitions.
For a love so free
will never fly away.

MINE BABE

I get butterflies,
every time,
you look at me, touch me, talk to me.
Big cheesy smiles across my face,
you fill that empty place,
deep in my heart,
where it has been lonely for such a long while,
I hope we never part.
Because if we did....
I don't know if I could take it..
I'm giving you my heart..
Please don't break it.
Oh I feel for you so much,
when your not with me
oh how I miss your touch.
I go crazy waiting for your reply,
when I can't talk to you I want to cry.
I don't think I've ever felt this way..
Feelings for you come more and more each and every day,
You know how to make me smile
I hate being away from you
even for a little while
you're so sweet
when I'm near you, my whole body fills with heat,
and I have an out of control heart beat.
I can't control myself
I can't help but want you all to myself.
I can't think of enough words to explain,
my feelings for you are simple, there plain.
Do you understand what I'm trying to say?
I'm so glad we found each other
I'm so glad we love one another.
There are only so many words to use to say
you are more then okay
you're mine babe.

MY WISH

A dream is a wish your heart makes,
and my heart made a wish for you,
that you may find a rainbow
where all your dreams will come true.

May there be sunlight ever streaming
into your heart each day,
may you find the bond of friendship
along each new highway.

May loving arms enfold you
when you need someone to care,
and may your heart know that my heart
is with you everywhere.

NEED YOU

The days go by so slow.
And the pain of missing you starts to show.
It's like all my excitment has been taken out of my days.
It's like all my happiness has been sucked down the drain.
And now it pours on me as cold unwanted rain.
What a desolate void I feel in my heart.
What a terrible pain I feel deep down inside.
That will only go away when you're by my side.

I need you.
I need you like I need the sun in the sky.
I need you like the water in the rivers flowing by.
There's a burning passion in your eyes that I need to see to survive.
I need you.

Living without you has made one thing clear.
And that is why I need you here.
I need you here right now,
'cause I can't live without you for too long.
So please come back and stay with me.
Please come back and laugh with me.
Please come back so you can see, that.

I need you.
I need you like I need the sun in the sky.
I need you like the water in the rivers flowing by.
There's a burning passion in your eyes that I need to see to survive.
I need you.

I need you with me, beside me so I can never let you go.
'Cause I love you more than you will ever know.
You're what I've been living for most of all.
You're what I need most of all.

I need you.
I need you like I need the sun in the sky.
I need you like the water in the rivers flowing by.
There's a burning passion in your eyes that I need to see to survive.
I need you.
I need you so bad!
I need you........

NO I WITHOUT YOU

No I without you,
I once had a life that you were not in,
and everyday it fell apart again and again.
But now I've found you
and our love is so true
I can't imagine my life without you!

Sometimes we get mad
sometimes we get sad
but we always make it through
because there is no I without a you!

Sometimes things get rough
and we both huff and we puff
but we always get through
because there is no I without a you!

When things get bad and we both make it through
because there is no I without a you!

So when we make it through
and we both say I love you!
It'salways because there is no I without a you!

ONE MOTHER

Hundreds of stars in the sky,
hundreds of shells on the shore together.
Hundreds of birds that go singing by,
hundreds of lambs in the sunny weather.

Hundreds of dewdrops to greet the dawn,
hundreds of bees to greet the clover.
Hundreds of butterflys on the lawn,
but only one mother special enough to be called,
MOM!!!

ONE WHO ALWAYS LOVES YOU

Maye I should go,
before my feelings show,
and tell you I can't
live without you.

Sunshine fills your room,
it always comes too soon,
and night time always leaves
my lonely.

But you make everyone
feel brand new,
with the things you say
and do,
that's why everybody
loves you.

And stars would shine
for just awhile,
if they didn't see
your smile,
or the heavens
that surround you.

So, I'll just let you sleep,
and in my dreams I'll keep,
a life with you I know
will never be.

But if someday you find,
I'm passing through your mind,
remember me as one
who always moves you.

ONLY LOVE YOU

From the moment that you caught my eye.
You stirred something inside me, that I can't deny.
This feeling inside me, makes me a little uneasy.
I'm suddenly dizzy and feeling a little bit queasy.

The sound of your voice, the sight of your smile.
Caused me such happiness, that I haven't felt in quite awhile.
From that day on, as we've grown closer.
I've felt the need for this verse, of which I'm the composer.

As each day passes, and the years fly by.
I've never had to ask, or even wonder why.
I knew at that moment, I wanted you for my wife.
My soul mate, with which I would spend the rest of my life.

So as I close, I hope you remember.
As my life fades, and the fire is now embers.
Looking below, from this heavenly pinnacle view.
Just think of these words, always and forever
I will only LOVE YOU!!!!

PERFECT

All I ever wanted was to be part
of your heart
and for us to be together to
never be apart.
No one else in the world could even compare,
you're perfect and so is this love we share.

We have so much more then I ever
thought we would,
I love you more then I though
I ever could.
I promise to give you all
I have to give,
I'll do anything for you as long
as I live.
In your eyes I see our present, future, and past,
by the way you look at me
I know we will last.
I hope that one day you will come to realize,
how perect you are when seen through my eyes.

POET'S LOVE

There is no raging sea
no sense of knowing reality
no fierce stab of intensity
poets' love is tranquility

A poets' love is sweet lotus leaves
and cherry garlands which dance atop streams
a drifting feel of sweet run water
which gives impressions of comforts dreams
dance on air to a poets musing
sweet illusive heartbeats thrill to the sense
soft smiles are in loves' secret
soft colors and feelings is loves' commence

Sweet heart has no war
no density to soft hearts' core
only giving, that's for sure
lotus leaves float to shore

In silent night are heartbeats heard
as loves' face alters thoughts' hardened air
mystic shapes do all transform
to generate sweet calling dreams affair
smile is sotened to effect
knowledge, that poetic love is compelling
reality must lose concentration
if sweet poetic love is love-hearts' selling

Poets' love, romantic dream
pastoral in tender scheme
painted as a loving theme
love is what love should seem.

RACISM

Of human ignorance I am almost in despair
for racism is around me everywhere
but like they say sheer ignorance is bliss
just like Judas betrayed Jesus with a kiss.

Some people carry their honour in a flag
and of their Nationality they brag
they feel superior and they differentiate
and against those who are diferent they discriminate.

So many people still judged by their race
for such there never ought to be a place
'A fair go' those untruthful words I do recall
there is no such a thing as a 'fair go for all'.

Though we live in a so called democracy
of racism we never will be free
They judge you by where you come from and the colour of your skin
for many equality and respect seems impossible to win.

It's been awhile since the days of Martin Luther King
his name to it has a familiar ring
If against racism he did not choose to strive
today the great man he would be alive.

So many holding the reins of power not spiritually aware
and racism is around me everywhere
and racism only leads to division and war
just goes to show how ignorant some are.

REDNECKS

Rednecks are simple,
we don't worry about pimples.
We all have guns,
so don't even try to run.
We go fishing all day,
while we drink the time away.
We love all our women,
we all love to go swimming.

Rednecks enjoy muddin',
and love banana puddin'.
We enjoy bbq's in our yards,
we always have our dogs on guard.

A shotgun in our truck,
on our wall a stuffed buck.
In our garage a jacked up chevy,
by our pond a well built levee.
We host square dances and hoe downs,
everyone of us were class clowns.
Until next time we raise our glasses,
I propose to all the rich people, kiss our asses!

ROLLING STONE

For those who have lost someone
in your life,
it cuts into your heart
just like a knife.

Feels like you're choking
 in an open space,
feels like you're cornered
in every place.

I'm here to tell you
that you're not alone,
but now you must carry on
like a rolling stone.

SAVING ANGEL

You come to me when I needed you the most,
you were a gift from God.
I treasure you each and everyday.
I would do anything for you, including give my life to save yours.
You are the most amazing woman I have ever known.
I am so blessed that you are a part of me.
I will spend forever trying to say thank you for saving me.
You may not know what it is you do for me,
I don't know where to begin telling you.
       You make my life worth living,
       you are the reason I get up every day,
       you are the reason I do everything that I do.
There are many more reasons why, but, the most important one is
that you love me.
You are my saving Angel sent here from God,
and I will cherish you for all time.

SEX

With the title of your poem,
you need the right hook.
Get the readers attention,
so, they will have a look.
Stimulate their curiosity,
something that will attract.
A very pleaseurable interest,
and you're on the right track.
Some words are like magic,
belonging to a certain list,
will capture many readers.
They are too hard to resist.
Titles should be in the poem,
it's what everyone expects.
So, I came to the decision,
and called this poem sex.

SHE IS

She gives me these feelings,
I've never felt before.
She promised me today,
and forever more.

She said she'll never leave,
I hope that's really true.
She had my heart when she said,
Baby, I love you.

She makes me feel so happy,
this feeling I can't compare.
She said whenever I need her,
that she'll always be there.

She gives me reasons to believe,
that life will come together.
She said that she will always hold me,
today, tomorrow, and forever.

She is someone I'll want to keep,
and never fathom letting go.
She is the one sent here for me,
I don't doubt her, because I know.

She's the only person,
whose heart I'll forever keep.
She is the only one,
whose kisses put me to sleep.

She is the one that promised me,
she will never leave.
She is the one that gives me,
every reason to breathe.

She's the one that can make,
my heart beat faster and slower at the same time.
She is the one I'm proud to say..
Will always and forever be mine.

SPECIAL DELIVERY

Ink spills upon paper mixed with tears,
memories of you reappear.
Years go by slowly since you are gone,
your sweet memory lives on.

An open book, my heart upon my sleeve,
silently inside I grieve.
I miss you more with each passing year,
wishing you still were here.

You look down seeing the words I write,
heavenly angel of the night.
Sister's love fills pages line after line,
written from this heart of mine.

When I can't go on you make me strong,
pick me up when the day is too long.
In my thoughts I wish I may wish I might,
have you here one more night.

Don't worry, till we meet again I'll be okay,
friends, family send love your way.
Mr postman, special delivery to heaven's gate,
down the path to glory interstate.

STARING AT YOU

I just stop and stare at you at random moments
just thinking of how beautiful you are to me
memories of everything you do flood into my mind at that time
the way you walk, your laugh, that smile of yours that every time I see it I fall deeeper

When I hold you in my arms, our bodies so close
there is a connection there that I never want to be broken
when I look into your eyes, my heart starts to soar
my heart skips a beat and my love for you grows even more

The love we share is one that is so rare
so precious and so whole
diamonds, pearls, rubies and gold become nothing
but average everyday stones in comparison

Because this love can't be captured or stolen
traded or bought or even completely put into words
but it can be seen by the way we look at each other
the way we caress, the way it just is between you and me

I see our love in everything we do
I feel our love, through our kisses, our touch
I see myself being with you and loving you for years to come
whenever it is that I just get lost staring at you...my love

TEARDROPS

What does God do with
all the teardrops left
by me and you?

Does He save them up for us
until our time on earth is through?

Does He use them to make rain,
waterfalls, rivers, and lakes?

Does He give them back so
we can cry another day?

Whatever He does, please always remember,
no matter what, He is always there
to take them away!

TEARS

Every teardrop tells a story,
as it's raining down our cheek.
The sound it makes cannot be heard,
for its voice is much to weak.

Listen to a teardrop fall,
but listen with your soul.
The silence screams of broken hearts
a sound you can't console.

Teardrops are a language
that's spoken from the heart.
An endless stream of liquid pain,
that hurts right from the start.

Tears are often misunderstood
as a cleansing of the soul,
but they leave scars that go unseen
when the pain begins to flow.

Tears are filled with part of us,
a part we try to hide.
They can come from many places
to show what's hidden inside.

Every teardrop tells a story,
that most will never hear.
For they don't understand the language
that's spoken by a tear.

THE NIGHT BEFORE

'Twas the night before hunting season, and all through the woods
you could see camp sights with tents, and hunting goods.
The guys long underwear hung on branches of trees,
as they aired out silently in the nightly cold breeze.
The hunters told jokes, laughed and drank beer galore,
then turned to their buddies, and asked them for more.
While visions of big bucks roamed through their heads,
neither could they sleep, for some forgot their beds.
In time they would pass out, not a worry in the world,
except for Billy's huge fart that made the campfire swirl.
When suddenly they awoke to such a horrifying sound.
Each of them grabbing their chests, as their heart went pound, pound,
springing from chairs, hammocks, truck cabs, to their feet,
they went to investigate, some of them white as sheets.
To their amazement there stood a magnificent beast.
One so cunning, its presence could make them cease,
it was a hell of a woman, dressed down in camo gear,
and with a rifle so quick... She was out to shoot OUR deer!
I knew something had to be done, and done right quick.
But with her strong stance I was afraid of this chick.
So with tears in our eyes, and frowns on our face,
we decided to give her some much needed space.
Surprisingly she hollered like that of a man (wo-man).
Come Dee-Dee, come on Flow, come girls we have to go,
with a righteous mud slinging truck they started bragging,
and all you could hear was the sound of them downshifting.
But before they got out of view I heard her exclaim (and loudly),
Good luck to all you hunters...for you won't forget this dame!

THE TEAPOT

An irate teapot blew off a little steam,
when all of a sudden he started to scream.
"The tea is now ready, aromatic and green
you had better remove it lest I make one big scene."
He was very short tempered and shouted a lot,
but just how would you act if you were always so hot?

TRUE LOVE

True love is a sacred flame
that burns eternally,
and none can dim its special glow
or change its destiny.

True love speaks in tender tones
and hears with gentle ears,
true love gives with open heart
and true love conquers fear.

True love makes no harsh demands
it neither rules nor binds,
and true love holds with gentle hands
the heart that it entwines.

UNCHARTED GROUND

Your body is uncharted ground,
that I want to map with my hands.
I want to feel every inch,
and every detail.

Your body is uncharted ground,
there are areas that have never been found.
I want to find every single spot,
that lifts you off the ground.

Your body is uncharted ground,
places that have never been touched.
I want to know every part of you inside and out,
including your heart.

Your body is uncharted ground,
I want to spend our lives
finding all the places that
make your head spin 'round!

VALENTINE

Please be my valentine,
not only on this day,
but everyday throughout the year.
You're my best friend in every way.
You are my box of chocolates,
in each piece a sweet surprise.
You shower me with diamonds,
with the sparkles in your eyes.
You are my valentine candy,
with the loving words your say.
You're like my dozen roses,
you are my heart's bouquet.
You touch me with tenderness,
that gently warms my heart.
You truly are my lifeblood,
I pray we'll never part.
You've given my life meaning,
like none other throughout my life.
You always bring me comort,
when my heart is filled with strife.
You are my ray of sunshine,
you're truly my best friend.
Our souls are joined together,
in a closeness that'll never end.
You'll always be my sweetheart,
beyond the end of time.
You give me so much happiness,
please be my valentine.

WET

My butt got wet
sitting in the grass next to the lake.

I was thinking of a poem.

I saw a duck
his butt was wet too.

I wonder what poem he's thinkg about.

WHAT I LOVE

What I love the most about you....

      When you first wake in the morning,
           you are still sleepy and a bit grumpy.
      When you get home from a long day of work,
           you are tired and have felt lonely.
      When we are watching a movie,
           you hide under the blanket when you get scared.
      When we are sitting outside,
           the way the light highlights your features.

What I love the most about you....

      You love me,
           for who I am,
           just the way I am.
      You don't judge anyone,
           for what they have done.
      You love with all your heart,
           you're not arfaid to let it show.

What I love the most about you.....

      Is that you are,
           simply you!

WHENEVER

Whenever you feel grieved,
full of sorrow, and looking to chat,
just call me, for I might be bored,
and want someone to laugh at.

WHOLE

For the times I have been weak,
you have carried me through.
For the times that I could not speak,
your words have held true.

In times of sorrow,
you make me believe
in a better tomorrow.

You have stolen my heart,
you give me life,
you have redeemed my soul.
Thanks to you
my world is now whole.

WISH YOU WERE HERE

My eyes are full of tears,
so much so, that they can no more see.

I wish you were here,
to chop these onions for me.

WITHOUT YOU

Me without you is like:
        The earth with no people,
        the sun with no light,
        the night with no starts.

A day without you is like:
        A year without rain,
        a week without thunder,
        a day without wind.

Baby, can't you see?
        You're all I need.
        Without you I may not survive this game we call life.

There's not one second in the day,
        that I don't think of you.
You make everyday worth my time.

Thinking of you is uncontrollable,
        missing you is indescribable.

Seeing you is a gift,
        oh babe, me without you is like
        a road with no end.

WOWMEN'S MOODS

An Angel of truth,
and a dream of fiction.
A woman is
a bundle of contradiction.

She's afraid of a wasp,
will scream at a mouse,
but will tackle her spouse
alone in the house.

Sour as vinegar,
sweet as a rose.
She will kiss you one minute
then turn up her nose.

She will win you in rage,
enchant you in silk.
She will be stronger than brandy,
then milder than milk.

At times she will be vengeful,
merry, then sad.
She will hate you like poison,
and love you like mad.

YOU KISSED ME

You kissed me goodnight!

I jumped out of breakfast,
and ate all my bed.

Put my hat on my coffee,
and my coat on my head.

Turned off the car,
hopped into the light.

All becuase,
        you kissed me goodnight!

YOU SHOWED ME LOVE

You've shown me what true love feels like,
made my empty life become whole.
You've made me into a better person,
happiness now fills my soul.

You told me I was beautiful,
each and every day.
I've never felt so worthy,
I'm speechless I must say.

You taught me how to love,
in a way so pure and true.
You somehow healed my broken heart,
I've fallen in love with you.

You took away the sorrow,
put happiness in it's place.
You've made me look forward to,
waking up each day to your face.

You made me believe that I,
could live a complete life.
I never thought I'd ever say this...
but I'm blessed to be a wife.

You give me reasons to believe,
that this love is here to last.
You taught me how to move on,
and no longer drown within my past.

You make my heart feel so much love,
I never thought I could ever feel.
You give me courage to believe,
that the love we have is very real.

You told me that our hearts will beat,
no longer separate, but always together.
You promised me I'll always have you,
from now until forever.

You took away my loneliness,
that consumed what was left of me.

You put back the pieces of my broken heart,
and now I live so happily.

YOU

I still remember the first day we met.
We were too shy to say much at all,
it's funny to think back to that time
because now we're having a ball!

They say that true friendship is rare,
an adage that I believe to be true.
Genuine friendship is something that I cherish
I am so lucky to have met you.

Our bond is extremely special,
it is unique in it's own way.
We have something irreplaceable,
I love you more and more each day.

We've been through so much together
in so little time we've shared.
I will never forget all the moments
that you've shown me how much you cared.

Friends are forever,
especially the bond that you and I possess.
I love your fun-filled personality,
somehow you never fail to impress.

The world could use more people like you
it would certainly be a better place.
I love everything about you
you are someone I could never replace.

You are always there for me,
when my spirits need a little lift.
I cannot thank you enough for that,
you are truly an extraordinary gift.

You are everything to me and more
I could never express that enough.
Life is such a treacherous journey, and
without you it would be even more tough.

Our story will continue to grow
with each passing day,

because I trust that with you by my side
everything will always be okay.

You are so dear to me
you know I will love you until the end.
I will always be there for you, and
you will always (and forever) be my best friend.

YOUR LIFE

Life is crazy and totally unpredictable.
It's going to push you over,
kick you while you're down and hit you when you try to get back up.
Not everything can beat you.
Things are going to change you,
but you get to choose which ones you let change you.
Listen to your heart, follow your dreams,
and let no one tell you what you're capable of.
Push the limits, bend the rules,
and enjoy every minute of it.
Laugh at everything,
live for as long as you can.
Love all, but trust none.
Believe in yourself,
and never lose faith in others, settle for nothing but only the best,
and give 110% in everything you do.
Take risks, live on the edge,
yet stay safe, and cherish every moment of it.
Life is a gift, appreciate all the rewards,
and jump on every opportunity.
Not everyone's going to love you but who needs them anyways.
Challenge everything, and fight for what you believe.
Back down to nothing, but give into the little things.
After all, that is what makes you.
Forget the unnecessary, but remember everything,
bring it with you everywhere you go.
Learn something new, and appreciate criticism,
Hate nothing, but dislike what you want.
Never forget where you came from,
and always remember where you are going.
Live life to its fullest, and have a reason for everything,
even if its totally insane.
Find your purpose in life and live it!
I'll be right here whenever you need someone to remind you,
that this is your life and you gotta live it the way
you want.

Melissa Edmunds

I have numerous poems published. I was born and raised in Wyoming and now live in New Mexico with my wife. I enjoy writing and have been doing it most of my life. I got a lot of inspiration from my brother, who is dearly missed. I hope you enjoy, thank you.

www.ingramcontent.com/pod-product-compliance
Lightning Source LLC
Chambersburg PA
CBHW081402280526
45788CB00009B/2965